12 GREAT TIPS ON WRITING TO PERSUADE

by Molly Jones

12 STORY LIBRARY

www.12StoryLibrary.com

Copyright © 2017 by Peterson Publishing Company, North Mankato, MN 56003. All rights reserved. No part of this book may be reproduced or utilized in any form or by any means without written permission from the publisher.

12-Story Library is an imprint of Peterson Publishing Company and Press Room Editions.

Produced for 12-Story Library by Red Line Editorial

Photographs ©: Donna McWilliam/AP Images, cover, 1; wavebreakmedia/Shutterstock Images, 4; principalli/iStockphoto, 5, 29; VectorLifestylepic/Shutterstock Images, 6, 28; flio/iStockphoto, 7; Monkey Business Images/Shutterstock Images, 8, 19, 24, 26; Ditty_about_summer/Shutterstock Images, 9; Syda Productions/Shutterstock Images, 10; IS_ImageSource/iStockphoto, 11; Zurijeta/Shutterstock Images, 12; Tuskegee University Archives/Museum, 13; quavondo/iStockphoto, 14; WestLight/iStockphoto, 15; Photographee.eu/Shutterstock Images, 16; Chris Schmidt/iStockphoto, 17; cosma/Shutterstock Images, 20; Pamela Moore/iStockphoto, 21; Lipskiy/Shutterstock Images, 22; Rido/Shutterstock Images, 23; zukerka/Shutterstock Images, 25; Steve Debenport/iStockphoto, 27

Library of Congress Cataloging-in-Publication Data
Names: Jones, Molly, 1933- author.
Title: 12 great tips on writing to persuade / by Molly Jones.
Other titles: Twelve great tips on writing to persuade
Description: Mankato, MN : 12-Story Library, 2017. | Series: Great tips on writing | Includes bibliographical references and index.
Identifiers: LCCN 2016002328 (print) | LCCN 2016004499 (ebook) | ISBN 9781632352798 (library bound : alk. paper) | ISBN 9781632353290 (pbk. : alk. paper) | ISBN 9781621434474 (hosted ebook)
Subjects: LCSH: English language--Rhetoric--Juvenile literature. | Persuasion (Rhetoric)--Juvenile literature.
Classification: LCC PE1408 .J8344 2016 (print) | LCC PE1408 (ebook) | DDC 808/.042--dc23
LC record available at http://lccn.loc.gov/2016002328

Printed in the United States of America

12 STORY LIBRARY

Access free, up-to-date content on this topic plus a full digital version of this book. Scan the QR code on page 31 or use your school's login at 12StoryLibrary.com.

Table of Contents

1 Choose a Topic

What do you care a lot about? Do you think your town should provide safe housing for people without homes? Are you convinced you should be elected president of the student council? Maybe, after a long school day, you believe homework assignments should be illegal.

Writing to persuade is a powerful way to change minds and bring about action. A persuasive writer is like a salesperson for an idea. The writer "sells" his or her knowledge about an issue. First, you must pick a topic. To get others to "buy" your opinion, the issue must be important to you. If you do not care about your subject, your readers will wonder why they should. Writing a good essay takes time and commitment. Picking a topic you are passionate about will help you write an essay you

Persuasive writing helps "sell" an idea.

are excited to complete and proud to present.

Brainstorming is a great way to think of topics. Often, we judge our ideas as good or bad. We reject those we don't think are useful. But when we brainstorm, we don't reject our ideas right away. We simply write down as many ideas as our brains can come up with—good or bad, silly or sensible.

Brainstorming is a good way to get ideas on the page.

Create a list of ideas. It might be clear which topic you want to write about right away. One might stand out as something you care a lot about. Other times, your topic will not be on your list. But the list might include an idea that makes you curious. After doing some research, you might find yourself becoming more and more interested in an issue from the list. Or your research might lead you to an exciting new topic.

Quick Tips

- Writing to persuade can help bring about big changes.
- Writers must care about their topics.
- Brainstorming is a great way to come up with a topic.

2

Get the Facts

The best way to learn about a topic is through research. Reading books in the library and articles on the Internet can supply you with lots of information. It is also good to interview one or more people who have experience with your topic. Their knowledge can help grow your understanding. They also may be able to answer questions you have about the topic.

Once you've started your research, be ready for surprises. What you learn may support your beliefs. But the information could also cause you to change your mind. If that happens, think of it as a good thing. Getting the facts has kept you from spreading wrong information.

As you research, take notes about what you learn. You can put your notes into three categories: one for general facts, one for data that support your original beliefs, and one that supports the opposite point of view. Be sure to include in your

Libraries are great places to start your research.

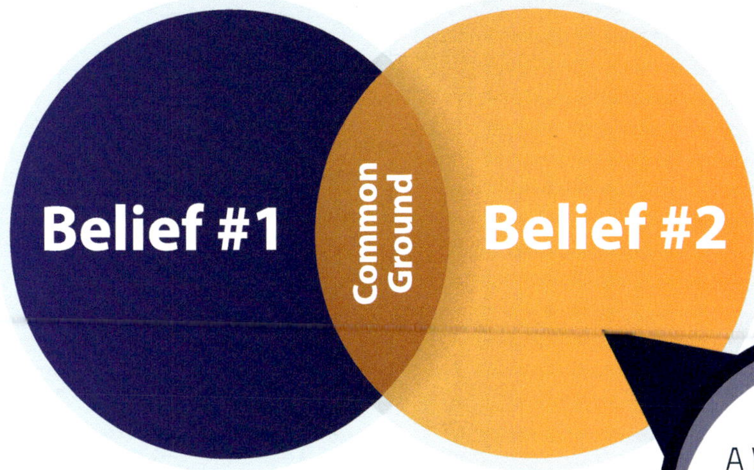

A Venn diagram can help you organize your notes.

notes where you get each piece of information. Organized notes will help you when you start writing.

Writing to influence is a big responsibility. Others will trust that what you say about the subject is true. It is important to get the facts straight with in-depth research. Before you begin to write, you should be able to answer *yes* to three questions:

1. Is my approach to the issue best for everyone?

2. Do I know the facts about all sides of the issue?

3. Am I prepared to answer questions from those who disagree with me?

TRY IT OUT

Suppose you believe your county should raise taxes to help pay for road repairs. Write a paragraph giving reasons why you might favor this. Write a second paragraph giving reasons why some people might be against it.

Quick Tips

- Understanding all sides of the issue is crucial.
- Experts can help fill gaps in your understanding.
- Your opinion may change during research.

3

Know Your Reader

You've done your research. Now, you need to think about who your readers will be. Suppose you want to write about your school's lunchtime rules. Students at your school are required to sit with the students from their class during lunchtime. But many students believe they should be able to sit with friends from other classes.

Maybe you support the students. In this case, your readers will be the school staff. Learn what their concerns are. You could speak with a staff member to find out why the rule was put in place to begin with.

Or maybe you hope to persuade students to accept the lunch rule. Then, you need to hear their concerns. In either case, you will want to show you understand both sides. You can then explain why your point of view will be good for everyone.

If you want to change your school's lunchtime rules, focus on the reasons behind the rules.

Keep track of what is most important to your readers.

You should also think about how much your readers will know about the issue. If you are writing for your school's staff, your readers will likely know the basics of the school-lunch rule. You may not need to spend as much time talking about general information. But if you are writing for your school's newspaper, your readers might not know much about the subject. You may need to spend more time giving the basics before going into the details.

Plan your writing to focus on the reader, not on yourself. Show why your viewpoint is best for everyone. Doing so will help readers feel confident in accepting your views.

TELLING BOTH SIDES

The following is an example of telling both sides of an issue:

> Many teachers support the lunch seating rule. They believe it helps ensure everyone has someone to sit with. They also say it helps students get to class on time after lunch. Students with good friends in their class tend not to feel strongly about the rule. But many students have spoken against it. They say the rule does not allow them to talk to their friends in other classes or meet new people.

Quick Tips

- Be sure your subject is one that will interest your readers.
- Plan to show you understand both sides of the subject.
- Focus on the readers' interests.

4

Organize Your Arguments

Many writers use the Rule of Three to organize their information. Having many arguments might seem like it would be better. But readers can have a hard time remembering the most important points if the information is not arranged simply. This does not mean you should limit the information in your essay. Instead, the information should be arranged to emphasize three main points. Plan to include an opening, a body, and a conclusion in your essay.

Imagine you are running for student council president. You are planning a campaign essay. It needs to convince students you are the best person for the job. In the opening, you want to introduce why you are writing. Remind readers that a student council election is approaching. Next, discuss the student body's common goal: a strong, effective student council. List the traits that make a good student council president.

Student councils make decisions for their schools' student bodies.

If you run for the student council, you will need to persuade others to vote for you.

Illustrate the traits by describing a successful former council president. Finally, outline the reasons why you too will be successful. Try to use three main points. For example, you might talk about your experience, your ideas, and your good relationship with the school staff.

In the body of your writing, give evidence that supports your claims. Give facts and statistics that you found during your research. You may also tell stories about yourself. For example, you might say how you have worked to change the school's lunch hour policy.

After the body of your essay, it is time to finish strong. Show you understand your opponent's strengths. But show how you are most likely to bring the biggest benefit to everyone. Remind your readers of the main goal—an effective student council.

Quick Tips

- Create an outline before writing.
- Apply the Rule of Three to organize your arguments.
- Finish by acknowledging the other view and stating why yours is better.

5

Write in a Narrative Style

You are now ready to start writing. But before you begin, it is important to think about writing style. Writing to persuade is a form of nonfiction writing. That means it tells true facts. But nonfiction does not need to be boring!

Nonfiction can be written in either a narrative or an educational style. Often, writers use both styles. But in either style, the writer is expected to make sure everything in his or her writing is true. Nothing is made up. Quotes are accurate. Events that are described really happened.

Writers often decide to write using a narrative style. This form of writing does more than just tell the facts. Like fiction, or made-up stories, narrative nonfiction starts with a strong character. Unlike fiction, the characters in nonfiction are real people. They exist now or existed in the past. Including a real character

Stories help readers engage in what they are reading.

in your nonfiction can stir your readers' emotions. It allows readers to identify more strongly with the topic. This can make your points more powerful. Before you begin to write, plan where it will be good to write in a narrative style and where it will be good to be more educational, or fact based.

WRITING STYLE

An example in educational style:

> In the early 19th century, many black people in the United States were enslaved. Often, slaves lived on their owners' land their entire lives. Most slaves never attended school.

An example in narrative style:

> George Washington Carver was born into slavery. Because he was black, he was not allowed to attend school. But Carver wanted so badly to learn to read that he sat outside the school door. He taught himself to read by listening to the lessons.

George Washington Carver was a famous scientist.

Quick Tips

- Narrative nonfiction tells true stories.
- Characters in nonfiction are real people.
- Using true stories helps readers connect with the writing.

6

Write with Active, Visual, and Precise Words

Effective words and phrases create images in readers' minds. They also make readers feel as though an action is taking place that they are a part of. Active voice helps make this happen.

In active voice, the subject of the sentence does the action. For example, "Mary won the election" is written in active voice. In passive voice, the subject is acted upon: "The election was won by Mary." Verbs that describe action, such as *run*, *jump*, *work*, *create*, *win*, or *drive*, are active. Passive verbs, such as *be*, *is*, *was*, and *were*, do not describe action. They are less likely to grab the reader's attention.

In addition to being active or passive, words can be precise or vague. For example, the phrase *two thousand five hundred* is precise. It is an exact number. The phrase *a large amount* is vague. It could

Dive and *catch* are active verbs.

Precise wording helps you place your meaning exactly where you want it.

mean many different numbers. Using precise words helps readers know exactly what you are saying. They help your message come across more strongly. For example, you might say, "I think Olivia would be a good choice for council president because she is a good person." But the sentence is stronger with more precise words. "Olivia would be an effective student council president because she works to make sure all students have a voice in school decisions."

A thesaurus may contain dozens of synonyms for the word *good*. They may range from *valuable* to *healthful* to *efficient*. Each of these expresses a different meaning. When you write to persuade, take time to say precisely what you mean.

Quick Tips

- Use words that create images in the reader's mind.
- Use active rather than passive voice.
- Find the word that expresses your precise meaning.

TRY IT OUT

Write two sentences using passive voice. Then rewrite the same sentences using active voice. How do the sentences sound different from each other?

7

Use Words That Persuade

For many people, persuasion is a full-time job. Whether persuading others to buy a product or to accept an idea, they are skilled at getting results. The aims of these people are not always genuine. But you can borrow the skills of persuasion to convince people of things you believe in.

One principle of persuasive language is that simple words pay off. You might assume complex words would impress readers. But longer words tend to require more thought. This tends to distract readers. The same rule applies with sentences. Readers can understand shorter sentences more quickly. Thus, they can grasp

Some people use persuasive techniques for their jobs.

Readers want to feel as though their concerns are being heard.

and remember your arguments more easily as they read. Simpler words and shorter sentences make readers more comfortable and more likely to be persuaded.

Another principle of persuasive language is to relate your argument to readers' lives. Words are more persuasive when they speak to what readers want. Always emphasize how your views would benefit your readers positively. Your writing will grab the reader's attention when it says more about his or her experience and less about your own. It is good to use more *you* and *your* words and fewer *I*, *me*, and *my* words.

FOCUS ON THE READER

Focusing on oneself can make readers lose interest in your goal:

> I don't like having to sit with my classmates at lunch. I have many other friends in other classes and would like to sit with them. Please sign my petition to change the school's lunch rules. It will give me the freedom to decide where to sit during my lunch hour.

The following example talks about a shared goal, which helps grab readers' interest:

> Please consider signing this petition about our cafeteria. If approved, you and other students could decide for yourselves where to sit during lunchtime.

Quick Tips

- Use simpler words when possible.
- Write in short sentences.
- Use more *you* and *your* words and fewer *I*, *me*, and *my* words.

8 Be a Positive Persuader

When writing to persuade, it's best to express yourself in a positive, friendly way. Doing so will help your readers be more open to your views. You may be writing about a controversial issue. Writing in a friendly way helps avoid creating bad feelings in readers who disagree with you. It keeps your readers open to hearing your ideas.

One way to avoid distancing readers is to stay away from generalizations. Words such as *everyone*, *nobody*, *always*, and *never* are often too simple. They do not show respect for other people's views. For example, do not say, "Everyone knows I am the best candidate for student council president." This type of statement may upset those who have questions about whether

STAYING POLITE

You do not need to put down others in order to persuade. A polite message can be just as strong:

> A student council president needs to get along with all students. But it is not enough to be popular. Good presidents must have good relationships with teachers and staff, too. They also need to be driven to make changes. It is our responsibility to pick a president we believe can make a difference. We have many fine candidates. But I believe you will see that I am the best person to lead the student body.

Being polite can make others more willing to listen.

you are the best person for the job. Instead, use information and examples to prove you are the right candidate.

Readers do not want to feel as though a writer is attacking them. They want to feel like the writer understands their perspectives. For example, it might be tempting to write, "The students in this school keep electing presidents who are popular but who have no skills to get the job done." But the tone of this sentence will make your readers feel like you are not on their side. Instead, write in a friendly, cooperative tone.

Quick Tips

- Be positive in how you express your views.
- Do not oversimplify others' positions.
- Do not attack your readers.

9 Make Good Transitions

Transitions are powerful tools for smooth, clear writing. Good transitions help fasten one idea to the next. They help your writing make sense. Suppose you're writing to influence your student body's vote on a new school schedule. Not using transitions can make it difficult to see how the sentences connect:

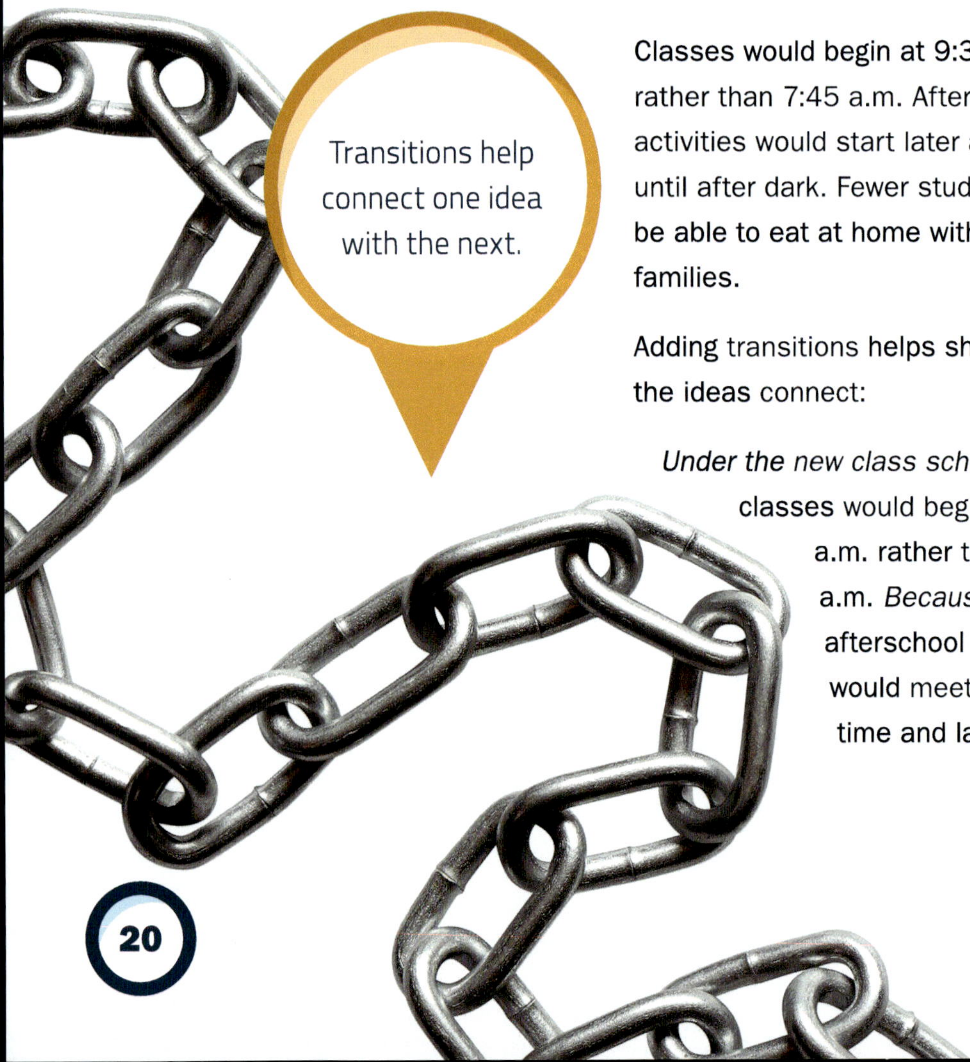

Transitions help connect one idea with the next.

Classes would begin at 9:30 a.m. rather than 7:45 a.m. Afterschool activities would start later and last until after dark. Fewer students will be able to eat at home with their families.

Adding transitions helps show how the ideas connect:

Under the new class schedule, classes would begin at 9:30 a.m. rather than 7:45 a.m. *Because of this,* afterschool activities would meet at a later time and last until

after dark. *If sports and clubs go later,* fewer students will be able to eat at home with their families.

Writers can choose from many transition words and phrases. As you read books and magazines, look for transition words. Think about how they clarify the passages in which they are used.

Quick Tips

- Transitions help smooth out choppy writing.
- Transitions help readers understand how sentences are related.
- Looking for transitions when reading can help strengthen your own writing.

TRY IT OUT

Rearrange sentences or add transitions to make this passage read more smoothly:

> Repairing potholes is costly. Trucks used to be prohibited on Main Street. Many huge trucks come down Main Street. Potholes have increased. The budget for road maintenance is used up.

10

Put the Finishing Touches on Your Piece

You have completed your persuasive essay. But you are not done yet. The next step is revision. All writers must revise their work, even professionals. It is essential to the writing process.

First, correct any spelling errors you have made. Use a spell-checker if you are writing on a computer. If you are writing by hand, use a dictionary to look up any words you are unsure of how to spell. Also, look up the meanings of any words you are not sure of.

Read over your entire piece. Imagine you are reading the ideas for the first time. Is all of the necessary information included for readers to understand your points? If not, add the missing pieces. Does the writing flow well from one idea to another? If not, work on fixing poor or missing transitions.

Next, read your writing aloud. Speaking the words can help you notice clumsy wording and repeated phrases. It is also good practice in

Use a dictionary to check spelling and word choice.

case you end up reading your work to an audience.

After improving wording where needed, ask another writer to read your work. This person will be more able to point out things that need to be clarified or other errors that have not already been corrected.

Quick Tips

- Check your spelling.
- Review your writing for smooth flow.
- Read your writing aloud to check for poor wording and repeated phrases.
- Have another person read your writing.

Share your work with others to get advice.

11

Give Credit to the Work of Others

Your writing likely contains thoughts and ideas from other writers. Their writing has helped you write a stronger essay. It is important to give them credit. You may have quoted others directly. Or maybe you just used their ideas. Either way, you need to list your sources.

Writers often list their sources at the end of their essays. Other times, writers use footnotes. Footnotes are marked with numbers that appear near the borrowed text. The source is documented at the bottom of the page next to the matching number.

Short quotes are sometimes acknowledged in the main text. For example, the text might say: "In his book, *Words That Work*, Frank Luntz describes his Ten Rules of Effective

A librarian or teacher can help you credit your sources.

Language." In this case, other documentation is not needed.

You should also show your sources when you include statistics. This gives credit to the people who collected the information. It also lets readers know where they can find the information on their own.

Quick Tips

- Give credit to others' ideas.
- Tell your readers where you found statistics.
- Include the sources in your notes so you can find them later.

Giving credit to others does not start after you have finished writing. It starts when you research. Keep notes of where you get your information when you research. This way, when you want to give credit to others, you know where you got the information.

Give credit to any work of other writers you've used in your writing. Someday, other writers may acknowledge using your work in their writings!

Keep track of where your information came from so you are not looking for it later.

12

Share Your Work

Writing is meant to be read. If your school doesn't have a writing group or club, seek out a teacher who would like to sponsor one. Reading one another's writing will help your communication skills. Also, look for opportunities to join a speaking group. Writing and delivering speeches offers great practice. It also gives you an opportunity to get feedback from others on your writing and delivery.

Be proactive. Ask your teacher or parent for help to find magazines and websites that publish the work of young writers. Read about what kind of work people are looking to publish. Choose those that fit what

Members of reading groups read each other's work.

Quick Tips

- Join a writing group.
- Submit your writing to places that publish student writing.
- Check with a teacher for ways to distribute your work.

TRY IT OUT

Make a list of three ways you can share your work. Consider publication opportunities and opportunities to read your writing in front of a group.

you have written. Then take action. Follow the guidelines for submitting your work. If your work is not selected to be published, read those that were selected. Then, write and submit again. That's what writers do who eventually get published: they read and they write every day.

Presenting your essay is a great way to persuade others.

Finally, consider distributing your work for others to read. A computer, a printer, and paper are all you need. When you write to persuade, getting your message to others is what's important. Check with a teacher about ways to get others to read your writing. Use all available methods to get your work read. Then start writing something new!

Writer's Checklist

✓ Decide on a topic you are passionate about.

✓ Be prepared: research your topic.

✓ Talk with experts on your subject.

✓ Know your readers and consider their needs.

✓ Organize your arguments into three main points.

✓ Include stories to make your writing more personal.

✓ Write in active voice rather than passive voice.

✓ Use your thesaurus to find the precise word to express your meaning.

- ✓ Write with simple words and shorter sentences.
- ✓ Use words that put the focus on the benefit to the reader.
- ✓ Use transition words to smooth out choppy writing.
- ✓ Have others read your writing to find ways it can be improved.

Glossary

active voice
When the subject of a sentence takes action.

controversial
A topic that brings about disagreement.

narrative
A written or spoken story.

passive voice
When the subject of a sentence is acted upon.

principle
A basic rule.

Rule of Three
A pattern of organizing items of information for easier learning.

statistic
A number that represents a piece of information.

synonym
A word that is similar in meaning to another word.

tone
The feeling or attitude expressed by someone.

transition
A shift in writing from one idea to another.

For More Information

Books

Benke, Karen. *Rip the Page! Adventures in Creative Writing*. Boston, MA: Trumpeter Books, 2010.

Forest, Christopher. *Present What You Know: Sharing Information*. North Mankato, MN: Capstone Press, 2013.

Guillain, Charlotte. *What is Persuasive Writing?* Chicago, IL: Heinemann Raintree, 2016.

Visit 12StoryLibrary.com

Scan the code or use your school's login at **12StoryLibrary.com** for recent updates about this topic and a full digital version of this book. Enjoy free access to:

- **Digital ebook**
- **Breaking news updates**
- **Live content feeds**
- **Videos, interactive maps, and graphics**
- **Additional web resources**

Note to educators: Visit 12StoryLibrary.com/register to sign up for free premium website access. Enjoy live content plus a full digital version of every 12-Story Library book you own for every student at your school.

Index

About the Author

Molly Jones, PhD, is author of 13 books of fiction and nonfiction as well as a number of magazine articles for young readers. She lives in the midlands of South Carolina.

READ MORE FROM 12-STORY LIBRARY

Every 12-Story Library book is available in many formats. For more information, visit 12StoryLibrary.com.